POLAR BEARS

Published by Creative Education, Inc., 123 South Broad Street, Mankato, Minnesota 56001

Library of Congress Cataloging-in-Publication Data

Biel, Timothy L.
Polar bears / Timothy Levi Biel.
p.   cm. — (Zoobooks)
Summary: Describes the physical characteristics, behavior, habitat, infancy, and future of the polar bear.
ISBN 0-88682-414-1
1. Polar bear—Juvenile literature. [1. Polar bear.] I. Title. II. Series: Zoo books (Mankato, Minn.)
QL737.C27B46   1991   599.74'446—dc20   91-8086 CIP AC

POLAR BEARS

This Book Created by
Quality Productions, Inc.

Written by
Timothy Levi Biel

Editorial Consultant
John Bonnett Wexo

Zoological Consultant
Charles R. Schroeder, D.V.M.
Director Emeritus
San Diego Zoo &
San Diego Wild Animal Park

Scientific Consultants
Dr. Douglas DeMaster
Leader, Marine Mammal Assessment Investigation
National Marine Fisheries Service

Dr. Ian Stirling
Canadian Wildlife Services

Creative Education

Art Credits

Main Art: Michael Woods; **Pages Eight and Nine:** Michael Woods; **Page Eight:** Raul Espinoza; **Page Nine:** Pamela & Walter Stuart; **Pages Ten and Eleven:** Michael Woods; **Page Ten: Top Left,** Lewis Sadler; **Top Right,** Pamela & Walter Stuart; **Page Eleven: Top Left,** Lewis Sadler; **Top Right,** Pamela & Walter Stuart; **Pages Twelve and Thirteen:** Walter Stuart; **Page Twelve:** Pamela & Walter Stuart; **Page Thirteen:** Rebecca Bliss; **Pages Sixteen and Seventeen:** Michael Woods; **Page Sixteen: Top,** Pamela Stuart; **Bottom,** Pamela & Walter Stuart; **Page Twenty:** Michael Woods; **Page Twenty-one: Top,** Ed Zilberts; **Bottom,** Pamela & Walter Stuart.

Photographic Credits

Cover: Mark Newman (Tom Stack & Associates); **Pages Six and Seven:** E. R. Degginger (Bruce Coleman, Inc.); **Page Eight:** George W. Calef (Photo Researchers); **Page Nine:** William Boehm; **Page Twelve: Bottom Left,** John Gerlach (Tom Stack & Associates); **Bottom Middle,** Tom McHugh (Photo Researchers); **Bottom Right,** Bob & Clara Calhoun (Bruce Coleman, Ltd.); **Pages Fourteen and Fifteen:** Wayne Lankinen (DRK Photos); **Page Sixteen:** Rod Allin (Tom Stack & Associates); **Page Seventeen: Top,** Margot Conte (Animals Animals); **Middle,** Margot Conte (Animals Animals); **Bottom,** Bob & Clara Calhoun (Photo Researchers); **Pages Eighteen and Nineteen:** Wayne Lankinen (Bruce Coleman, Ltd.); **Page Eighteen, Top,** Jack Fields (Photo Researchers); Bottom, **Dan Guravich (Photo Researchers); Page Nineteen: Top,** Margot Conte (Animals Animals); **Bottom,** William Boehm; **Page Twenty-one: Top,** Shostal Associates; **Bottom,** Ward Will (FPG Photo); **Page Twenty-two and Inside Back Cover:** David C. Fritts (Animals Animals).

Our Thanks To: Jack Lentfer (Alaska Department of Fish & Game); Susan Breisch (San Diego Museum of Natural History); Hugh Evans (Milwaukee County Zoo); Sarah George (Los Angeles County Museum); Michaele Robinson and Janet Lombard (San Diego Zoo Library); Mrs. Reynolds (San Diego Public Library); Deanna Leonhardt, Marjorie Shaw.

Contents

The polar bear is king of the north. It reigns over a world of snow, ice, and water, where most animals cannot survive. There *are* other animals that live here also, such as seals, walruses, foxes, and geese. But the biggest, strongest, and fiercest of them all is the polar bear.

Among land animals, the polar bear is the largest predator in the world. Standing on its rear legs, it is tall enough to look an elephant in the eye! The biggest polar bear ever measured was a male that stood more than 11 feet tall (3.3 meters) and weighed nearly a ton (900 kilograms). An average male weighs *only* one thousand pounds (450 kilograms), and females weigh about half that much.

Despite their enormous size, polar bears are graceful and athletic. They jump over cracks in the ice more than 20 feet wide (6 meters). They climb snow banks and steep ridges of ice. They are also expert long-distance swimmers, and are often seen in the Arctic Ocean several miles from shore.

Polar bears look like other bears, except for a few obvious differences. They have white fur, made especially to keep them warm. They have narrower heads, smaller ears, and longer teeth than other bears. In these and other ways, polar bears are built to live and hunt in the frozen Arctic.

Most of a polar bear's life is spent hunting for food. Its favorite food is seal blubber. A polar bear wanders far and wide in its search for seals. Yet even when it finds them, they aren't easy to catch. This bear uses many different techniques to hunt seals. But most often, the seals get away, and the polar bear must continue its lonely search.

Polar bears live and hunt alone, except when they are cubs. It takes a young polar bear about 3 years before it is big enough to live and hunt without its mother. Once it is full grown, a polar bear is safe from almost anything—except other polar bears, and humans. If they escape these dangers, polar bears may live long lives. In fact, a polar bear once lived in the London Zoo for 41 years.

Polar bears live at the top of the world. This icy region from the North Pole to the northern coasts of Europe, Asia, and North America is called the *Arctic*. Most of the Arctic is ocean, and much of it is covered with ice.

Polar bears usually live on the ice. They use it as a platform for stalking seals. But the amount of ice in the ocean changes from summer to winter, so the polar bears must migrate. Most of them travel to the same summer and winter areas year after year.

Polar bears do not always travel over land or ice. They are strong swimmers and can easily swim *more than a hundred miles (170 kilometers)* without stopping to rest.

The summer and winter ranges of polar bears are shown by the yellow areas on the maps below. In the summer, the ice in the southern part of the Arctic Ocean melts. Then most polar bears travel north to stay on the ice. But there is not enough ice for them all. So some polar bears head south to spend the summer on land.

In the winter and spring, ice forms over most of the Arctic Ocean. Polar bears come down from the North to hunt on this new ice. And those living on shore go north for the same reason.

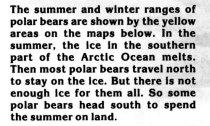

NORTH POLE

ARCTIC OCEAN

SUMMER RANGE

NORTH POLE

ARCTIC OCEAN

WINTER RANGE

Polar bears live on ice, but only where they can find seals. For example, the area nearest the North Pole is covered with a solid sheet of ice Ⓐ. But very few seals live this far north, so you won't find many polar bears here either.

Ⓐ

Ⓑ

Farther south, the ice breaks into huge "islands" Ⓑ. This is where most seals live, and most polar bears too. Every bear has a hunting territory, shown here as the dark orange area in the middle. If it can't find enough seals in its own territory, the polar bear will wander over a larger area, as shown in light orange.

Ⓒ

When they migrate, polar bears often travel hundreds of miles. But they usually return each year to the same areas where they learned to hunt as young cubs.

Ice also forms along the shorelines in the winter Ⓒ. This is where most female seals come to have their babies. And in early spring, many polar bears come here to hunt for seals.

In summer, when the ice melts, some polar bears come ashore. For a few months, they act just like brown bears, staying in the forests and eating wild berries.

Mother polar bears and their cubs usually spend the winter in dens on land. In the spring, they return to the ice to hunt seals. This mother is teaching her cubs to hunt.

9

The body of a polar bear is made for living in the cold. In fact, polar bears like the cold. They are so good at staying warm that they get uncomfortable even on slightly warm days.

For one thing, polar bears have large bodies. And large bodies usually hold heat much better than small bodies. But the large body of a polar bear also has extra layers of protection against the cold.

Unlike other bears, polar bears get most of their food by hunting. That's because there aren't many plants to eat where polar bears live. Fortunately, polar bears are extremely powerful, and they have many features that help make them excellent hunters.

QUESTION: **Of the two outfits shown at left, which one would keep you warmest in a cold wind? Which one would be best for keeping you warm in the water?**

ANSWER: **A parka, of course, would keep you nice and warm in the cold wind.**

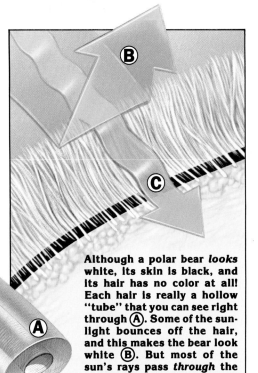

Although a polar bear *looks* white, its skin is black, and its hair has no color at all! Each hair is really a hollow "tube" that you can see right through Ⓐ. Some of the sunlight bounces off the hair, and this makes the bear look white Ⓑ. But most of the sun's rays pass *through* the hollow hairs and are trapped by the bear's black skin Ⓒ.

FUR

SKIN

BLUBBER

A polar bear's front paws are its most dangerous weapons. Each one is like a 25-pound sledge hammer (11 kilograms) that the bear can swing with deadly force. The paw is also a "handy" tool. The large rough pad keeps the bear from slipping on the ice. And the short, sharp claws are just right for holding on to slippery prey.

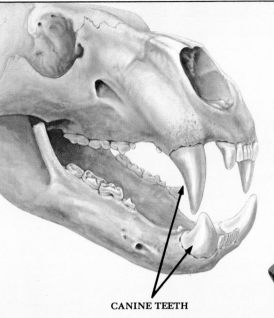

A polar bear has the long canine teeth and powerful jaws of a hunter. Unlike most predators, though, it does not usually use them to kill prey. After striking a seal with its paw, it uses its jaws and teeth to drag the seal out of the water.

The polar bear wears a "parka" *and* a "wetsuit." Its fur coat works like a parka. And just beneath its skin lies a rubbery layer of fat, called *blubber*, that works like a wetsuit. The blubber may be more than 4 inches thick (10 centimeters) in places, and it shields the bear's body from icy cold water.

CANINE TEETH

Polar bears have longer heads than other bears, and longer noses too. This gives them a superb sense of smell. Some people say they can smell a seal from more than 3 miles away (5 kilometers).

Although everything else about a polar bear is big, its ears are tiny. It doesn't need excellent hearing to hunt seals, because it uses a keen sense of smell instead. And besides, if the ears were bigger, they would stick out. And then they would quickly freeze.

This is one of the biggest and strongest animals in the world. Even its bones are heavy, because they have to support the weight of its bulging muscles. And did you notice the size of the polar bear's feet? The actual size of a single paw is about one foot wide (30 centimeters) and 18 inches long (45 centimeters).

Hunting on ice is not easy. And catching expert swimmers like seals is even harder. To catch them, a polar bear needs a keen sense of smell, a variety of hunting methods, and incredible patience.

First, it may have to walk or swim several miles just to find seals. Then it may find them lying on the ice, swimming in open water, or even swimming *under* the ice.

Wherever they are, the polar bear must be prepared to hunt them. As you see below, there are certain times of the year when the hunting is fairly easy, and other times when it is very difficult.

In the spring, most polar bears eat so much they get fat. This is when seals are easiest to find. So a polar bear may gain more than 200 pounds (90 kilograms)! This is just its way of storing food for later in the year, when hunting is not so easy.

In the fall and winter, the polar bear has to go on a diet. Seals are harder to find, so it doesn't have as much to eat. At this time, the polar bear's body begins using the extra fat that it stored up in the spring. So by late winter, the "fat" bear has become a "skinny" bear.

SNOW GOOSE

When polar bears can't find seals, they may try hunting other animals. They will hunt Snow Geese, like the one above, and they have also been seen feeding on beached White Whales, or *belugas* (buh-LOO-guz), like the one at right.

BELUGA

LEMMING

A polar bear will even hunt this tiny lemming. Think how strange it must look to see an 800-pound bear (365 kilograms) pouncing on a 2-ounce rodent (56 grams)!

With its keen sense of smell, a polar bear can sniff out a seal's *birth lair*. This is a den under the snow where seals have their babies. By spring, there may be 3 or 4 feet of ice and snow (1 to 1.3 meters) covering the lair. The polar bear pounds on the roof until it caves in. Then it enters the den headfirst to look for seals inside.

Sitting and waiting is the polar bear's most common method of hunting Ⓐ. It sits patiently beside a hole in the ice where it knows that a seal will come up for air. It may wait there for hours, but when the seal comes up, the bear must be alert. Then with lightning speed, it uses its gigantic paw to slap the seal.

A polar bear can also sneak up on a seal by *crawling* Ⓑ. First it lies flat on the ice like a big bear rug. Then it creeps slowly toward the seal.

Occasionally, a polar bear will attack *from the water* Ⓒ. First it swims noiselessly toward the seal.

When it gets close, it dives and approaches under water. At the last second, it springs to the surface and lunges at the surprised seal.

13

MOTHER AND CUB

Polar bear cubs stay with their mothers until they are almost 3 years old. During that time, the mother is as devoted and loyal as any mom can be. She finds food for them. She teaches them to hunt. She protects them, and if necessary, she will defend them with her own life.

A mother polar bear usually gives birth to two cubs in the middle of winter. At birth, the cubs are incredibly tiny. For 3 months, they must stay inside a warm den under the snow, where the mother gives them milk and keeps them warm.

A den dug out of the snow keeps mother and baby polar bears warm all winter long. To help keep out the cold, the den has a long entrance tunnel. And the mother often builds a mound of snow in front of the tunnel to block the wind.

Imagine how much growing a baby polar bear has to do! At birth, it weighs about one pound (450 grams). And it is small enough to hold in your hands. It cannot see or hear, and it has only a thin coat of white hair ①.

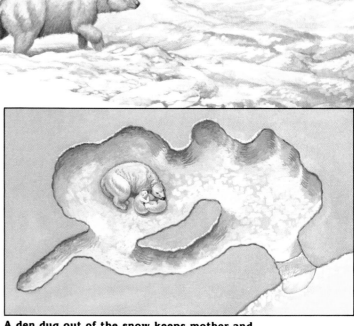

When a cub is 3 months old, it is finally ready to leave the den. But for several weeks, the little bear will hardly leave its mother's side ④.

① In the first month, a cub grows more than 4 times its original size. By the time it is a month old, it can see and hear, but it still cannot walk ②.

② A two-month-old cub weighs about as much as a newborn human. By this time, the cub knows how to walk, but it is still not strong enough to leave the den ③.

Young cubs will climb on their mother's back when they are frightened. They may be startled by a walrus, a human, or even another polar bear. But anything that threatens the cubs must face an angry mother. Female polar bears will fight with every ounce of their strength to protect their cubs.

A mother polar bear is a gentle giant. This mother sits patiently while her little one gets a drink of milk (above). Then she takes a little nap while junior plays on her back.

Cubs remain with their mothers until they are almost full grown. But even then they love to play. The two young bears on the right appear to be playing "hide and seek" with their mother.

17

We have much to learn about the ways of the polar bear. Until recently, few scientists traveled to the Arctic to study them in the wild. But today, as we learn more about polar bears, they continue to surprise and delight us.

People used to think that adult polar bears did not like one another's company. When they were seen together, they always seemed to be fighting. But now we realize that most of their fighting is just for fun.

There are still many unanswered questions about polar bears. We are just beginning to appreciate their wonderful variety of behaviors. In fact, we are often amazed by them because they seem to act almost human.

A polar bear often stands on its rear legs to look around and sniff the air. Standing like this, you almost expect it to raise a paw to its forehead, like a human explorer surveying the horizon.

Polar bears spend most of their time alone. They wander over the ice, hunting for seals. But sometimes they will just sit right down in the snow and do nothing. When they sit like this, they look like gigantic teddy bears.

When polar bears meet, they sometimes seem happy to see one another. They may wrestle and play for hours. And one of their favorite places to wrestle is in the water.

Polar bears have a tremendous curiosity —especially when they smell food. That is why so many of them visit the dump grounds in towns and villages throughout the Arctic. In fact, some of these dump grounds have become favorite sites for scientists to observe polar bears.

One of the most wonderful things about polar bears is the way a mother looks after her cubs. For nearly 3 years, a polar bear mother cares for her young the way a human mother cares for her children.

People of the North have lived near polar bears for thousands of years. They have hunted polar bears. But they have also learned from them. According to their legends, polar bears taught them how to hunt, travel, and stay warm.

Today, these people are becoming more modern. They are using modern tools and vehicles, and living in modern houses. But many of them have kept alive the same respect for the polar bear that their ancestors had.

People have long admired polar bears and featured them in their artwork. The sculpture at left shows a polar bear attacking a seal. People probably learned how to hunt seals by watching polar bears hunt.

Arctic people have learned how to make temporary snow huts, called *igloos*. A polar bear's den may have been the model for the first igloo.

People learned long ago that the thick fur of the polar bear kept them warm. The man at left is wearing a pair of pants made of polar bear fur. Modern scientists have still not invented a material as warm as this.

Many people in the Arctic still hunt polar bears in the traditional ways of their ancestors. Today, however, a snowmobile often replaces the team of dogs. But hunting the polar bear alone is still a test of courage.

According to legend, the polar bear has a spirit that is wise and strong. And when a hunter kills a polar bear, he honors its spirit by placing its skull in his window.

21

The future of polar bears depends on people, now more than ever before. Until recently, most polar bears and other arctic animals lived undisturbed by people. A few were hunted, but not enough were killed to threaten their future. The rugged climate kept most people away. And the Arctic remained the world's last unspoiled frontier.

Today, most of it is still unspoiled. But people are moving in. They are exploring the arctic wilderness with modern airplanes, ships, and snow machines. And they are discovering valuable natural resources, like gas and oil. Oil drills, pipelines, roads, and airstrips are being constructed. New towns are being built.

All this activity may be harmful to polar bears and other animals of the North. We know how industrial development has destroyed natural habitats in other parts of the world. If people aren't careful, they could destroy the Arctic in the same way.

Fortunately, polar bears are not in immediate danger. There are about 20 thousand of them living in the Arctic today. But they depend on seals for their survival. Seals, of course, depend on fish. And fish need plenty of plant life and clean water. Because so few plants and animals can live in this part of the world, it would be easy to upset the balance among them. So protecting the polar bear really means preserving the plants and animals on which it depends.

Concerned scientists, politicians, and business people are already trying to do that. All polar bears live in just 5 countries—the Soviet Union, Norway, Denmark, Canada, and the United States. The leaders of these countries have signed an internation agreement to protect the polar bear. They are working together to limit hunting, set aside wilderness areas, and study polar bear behavior.

This spirit of cooperation is making a difference. The world's largest national park has been established in northern Greenland, where many polar bears live. The other Arctic nations are also protecting large wilderness areas. In these protected areas, *all* natural resources—including the polar bear—are being saved for the future.

Index